T0203355

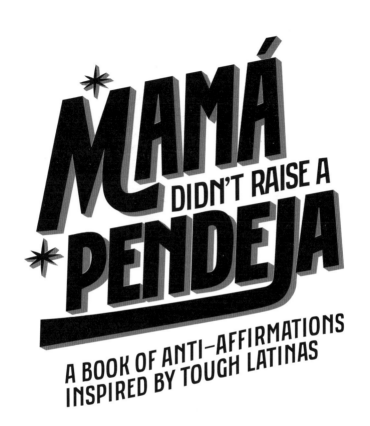

MAMÁ DIDN'T RAISE A PENDEJA

A BOOK OF ANTI-AFFIRMATIONS INSPIRED BY TOUGH LATINAS

ARALIS MEJIA & CAROLINA ACOSTA

Blue Star Press.

Illustrated by Niege Borges
Design by Bryce de Flamand
Author photographs by Emre Demir

ISBN: 9781963183078

Printed in Colombia

10 9 8 7 6 5 4 3 2 1

**To our badass moms
and abuelas**,
thank you for teaching us
and always reminding us
to be strong and resilient,
and to never let anyone
make us a pendeja.

Contents

Introduction

Welcome to *Mamá Didn't Raise a Pendeja*: your unfiltered guide to tackling life's messiest moments with the fierceness of a Latina matriarch. This isn't your typical self-help book sprinkled with fluffy affirmations and gentle nudges. Nope, we're throwing hard-hitting Spanish wisdom at you like a **chancla** to the face.

In these pages, we'll show you how to navigate through life's tricky waters, from dodging crypto scams to surviving family drama during the holidays. Each chapter unfurls a collection of Spanish sayings that our ancestors wielded like verbal machetes through the jungles of life. Accompanying each proverb is its direct English translation and a modernized version—an anti-affirmation, if you will—that'll have you armed and ready to face any **pendejada** with a smirk.

This book is more than just a collection of sayings. It's a love letter to our moms and the generations of strong, independent Latinas who shaped us. It's for anyone who's ever needed a swift kick to get moving, a reminder to own their actions, and the inspiration to hold their heads high. The wisdom within these pages will guide you through life's ups and downs, reminding you to grow, to fight—and most importantly—to never, ever let life make a *pendeja* out of you.

So what exactly is a *pendeja*? In the simplest terms, it's a fool—an idiot, really. In this book's title, we're using the feminine noun, referring to your two female authors, with the masculine noun being *pendejo*. The origins of the word trace back to sixteenth-century Spain, where it was used to describe overconfident teens who thought a few pubes made them adults. Today, it's a catchall term for anyone caught in a moment of stupidity. Our moms would say "*por pendeja*," or "for being an idiot," whenever we caused something unfortunate to happen to ourselves. That time nine-year-old Carolina busted a tooth running and falling down the stairs? *Por pendeja*. Or the other time fourth-grade Aralis lost her favorite lunch box after rushing off to play during recess?

Por pendeja. It's a loving way of reminding us that, yes, sometimes life hits hard—often directly from our own doing.

We, Carolina Acosta and Aralis Mejia, grew up under the watchful eyes of our formidable mothers—sisters who migrated from Colombia and brought with them a treasure trove of sayings that could snap you back to reality faster than you can say "***¡puta madre!***" These phrases, passed down from our ***abuela***—a woman as tough as they come—were not just advice; they were survival tools, guiding our ancestors through generations.

Our mothers, Martha Lopez née Garcia and Nidia Aragon, were the embodiment of resilience and strength. Born in Colombia, they both took brave leaps of faith, moving to new countries in pursuit of better lives for themselves and their families.

Carolina's mother, Martha, was born in Palmira, Colombia, the youngest of six children. At thirteen, she followed her eldest sisters to Montreal, and later, at eighteen, she joined her sister Nidia in New York City, where she met Carolina's father. Two kids, a divorce, and another marriage later, Martha became the version of the mom Carolina remembers most vividly—a responsible, fun, and independent woman who never took shit from anyone.

Aralis's mother, Nidia, moved to New York City in her early twenties, driven by the hope of creating a better life. Despite the challenges she faced, including raising Aralis and her sister on her own after leaving a toxic relationship, Nidia poured her heart and soul into giving her daughters a childhood filled with love and stability.

Growing up, we learned three permanent lessons from our mothers. First, never half-ass anything. If you say you're going to do something, give it your all or don't even bother starting. This drive has empowered us to excel in our careers and entrepreneurial pursuits. Second, always be presentable. Our mothers—sexy Colombians who wouldn't be caught dead without a face of makeup and fine jewelry—taught us the importance of confidence and carrying ourselves with pride. Finally, and most importantly, never let anyone disrespect you. Seeing our mothers stand up for themselves, especially to men, had a profound impact on the development of our own self-respect.

Inspired by the toughness we learned at home, we've both ventured into entrepreneurship. Carolina founded Tragos Games, a best-selling drinking game for Latinos currently sold in Target and Walmart stores and on other major online retailers. Aralis started her own marketing agency, Silara Inc., and expanded into real estate, successfully investing in and managing multiple properties. Our mothers' faith in our abilities and support in our career choices made it much more comfortable for us to take these risks.

Here's to incredible women like our mothers—let's celebrate them, learn from their stories, and be inspired to lead our lives with as much bravery and determination. We hope you find laughter and wisdom in the anti-affirmations featured throughout this book. Embrace them as daily mantras—as they've become ours—to fortify your positivity and confidence as you face each day's blessings and challenges.

Hey there, non-Spanish speakers!

We know that not everyone is a master of **español**, or Spanish—and that's okay! At the back of this book, you'll find a glossary that'll help you navigate any Spanish words and phrases you don't recognize. Think of it as your personal interpreter. So, whenever you come across a word that makes you scratch your head, just flip to the back and let our glossary be your guide.

Stay Sharp, Stay Ready

In this chapter, we're tapping into *abuela's* no-BS wisdom to keep you sharp and on your toes. From cutting toxic ties to dodging bad advice, these hard-hitting truths are all about staying ready for whatever comes your way. Get ready for some real talk that'll keep you one step ahead, always.

Soldado advertido no muere en guerra.

DIRECT TRANSLATION

A warned soldier does not die in war.

MODERN TRANSLATION

Hope for the best, but plan for the worst!

Latina moms are the queens of **por si acaso**, or "just in case," always preparing for the worst. "Take a sweater **por si acaso** you get cold!" (It's ninety degrees outside.) "Avoid parked vans **por si acaso** there's a kidnapper waiting inside!" (Jesus!) And the classic, "Get to the airport three hours early **por si acaso** you forget your passport." *Cue eye roll.* But, they were onto something!

Soldado advertido no muere en guerra. Keep spare underwear handy in case of . . . accidents. Sample your friend's "mild" guac cautiously. (Their definition of "mild" might be "sets your mouth on fire.") And share your location before that first Tinder date in case you end up in a *Law & Order* episode. *Dun-dun.* This seemingly paranoid mom-mindset can save your ass when you least expect it!

A burro negro, no le busque pelo blanco.

DIRECT TRANSLATION

Don't look for a white hair on a black donkey.

MODERN TRANSLATION

Don't waste time looking for the good in something toxic.

If you're constantly giving people or circumstances the benefit of the doubt, then this saying is a reminder for you to *stop*! Too often, we ignore the red flags when trying to make things work—out of comfort or fear of change. Who or what in your life are you making too many excuses for?

¡A burro negro, no le busque pelo blanco! Stop trying to turn that fuck boy into a faithful partner! His actions are showing you his true colors and they're all shades of hell no. And that stressful job you've held on to, hoping for a raise after four years—it's time to update that resume and get the hell out. Ditch the things that are taking up unnecessary space in your life!

A palabras necias oídos sordos.

DIRECT TRANSLATION

To foolish words, deaf ears.

MODERN TRANSLATION

Some advice is shit. Not all advice is worth listening to.

Colombians call people who share their opinions even when they don't know what they're talking about **habladores**, which translates to "talkers." Even if people have good intentions, you're not required to engage with every bit of their nonsense.

By giving attention to foolish words, you're just bestowing power to them that they don't deserve. Your single **tía's** unsolicited dating advice? In one ear and right out the other! Your coworker's "foolproof" strategy for getting rich quickly with cryptocurrency? **¡A palabras necias, oídos sordos!** Stay wary of irrelevant and uninformed advice that could lead you astray.

Toda el agua de la boca no se bota.

DIRECT TRANSLATION

Don't spill all the water in your mouth.

MODERN TRANSLATION

You don't have to share all your shit.

When it comes to your own matters, shut your damn mouth! Our **mamás** taught us that we should always be cautious with anything we tell people because **uno nunca sabe** what energies they might send your way, intentionally or not.

Toda el agua de la boca no se bota. Your coworkers don't need to know every detail of your love life! That's how you end up as the topic of conversation on all of those secret Slack chats. And your nosy neighbor doesn't need to know about your recent raise or bonus. They'll know soon enough once you pass by them with that Louis Vuitton on your arm. So keep some things close to the chest; they're always safest with you.

Más vale pájaro en mano que cien volando.

DIRECT TRANSLATION

A bird in the hand is worth one hundred flying.

MODERN TRANSLATION

The best opportunity is the one you'll actually pursue.

Don't spend all your time waiting for the perfect opportunity to fall into your lap. It may be tempting to daydream about greater things—a job where your boss doesn't make you feel like a total **idiota**, an apartment with an in-unit washer and dryer (we're not all blessed!), a partner who looks like **Maluma**—but ask yourself: are you doing what it takes to reach those bigger aspirations or just dreaming about what-ifs?

Más vale pájaro en mano que cien volando. The grass isn't always greener on the other side; it's greenest where you water it. So focus on growing the potential of what's within reach, because we all have some untouched seeds to plant!

¡Zapatero, a sus zapatos!

DIRECT TRANSLATION
Shoemaker, to your shoes!

MODERN TRANSLATION
Mind your freakin' business!

Focus your emotional energy on your own problems, and only speak on topics that you are truly passionate about or educated on. Don't know a thing about the stock market? Then stop telling your friend to invest in triple-leveraged funds because three must be better than one! Your two coworkers' not-so-secret hookup sesh in the maintenance closet? Stay out of it unless you want to get caught in the drama when they inevitably break up and start throwing jabs during work meetings.

Cierra el pico, and lend an ear instead. Becoming too involved or voicing your opinion on something that has nothing to do with you will only make you look like an ignorant ***metida***. So ¡***zapatero, a sus zapatos***! Save yourself the trouble and stay in your lane.

No hay más sordo que el que no quiere oír.

DIRECT TRANSLATION

There is no one more deaf than he who does not want to hear.

MODERN TRANSLATION

You can't force someone to listen.

We all know that hard-headed person who vents about problems we've repeatedly given them advice on. No matter how much you want to shake some sense into them, you can't force them to do anything, even if it's for their own well-being. They've got to be ready to change on their own.

No hay más sordo que el que no quiere oír.

You can tell our friend Aylin a million times to let go of the same **tóxico** who always leaves her on read. But, she'll have to decide when she's ready to drop his ass. You can teach our Tío Hernan how to upload a photo on Facebook each week, but somehow he'll always end up signing himself out of his account instead. So when it comes to the stubborn, sometimes all you can do is sit back and stay out of it.

Guarda el orden que el orden te guardará a ti.

DIRECT TRANSLATION

Keep the order and order will keep you.

MODERN TRANSLATION

Habits will make or break you!

Our **mamás** ran a tight ship: make our beds every morning, do homework right after school, wash our dishes right away. Laziness wasn't tolerated, and the phrase "I'll do it later" was unheard of unless you wanted to get the **chancla**. Despite fear tactics, these habits helped us maintain organization, stability, and cleanliness. **¡Como debe de ser!**

Guarda el orden que el orden te guardará a ti. Creating order makes for a more resilient and prepared mind when things don't go as planned. It may seem daunting, but start small. Can't stay steady at the gym? Start by going once a week. Room constantly looking like a Goodwill donation corner? Just make the bed every day. Those small steps will help you build a solid foundation of permanent good habits. Eventually, you may even see your floor again!

El que pone dos ollas al fuego, una de las dos se quema.

DIRECT TRANSLATION

If you put two pots on the stove, one of the two will burn.

MODERN TRANSLATION

You're not a tortilla, so don't burn yourself out!

Overachievers, listen up! We love that "I can do it all" attitude, but let's be real—you're no superhero. You're more like a pressure cooker about to explode. *Alexa, play the *Encanto* soundtrack song "Surface Pressure."* It's easy to lose sight of your priorities when cooking too many things at once, and eventually, something's gonna burn (probably your sanity)! Don't be surprised when ¡**todo se va a la chingada**!

El que pone dos ollas al fuego, una de las dos se quema. Joining a book club while moving and starting a new job? Not advisable. Juggling multiple Hinge baes to really test the waters? Now that's just asking for trouble! Don't overcommit and overextend yourself. Instead, focus on what matters most by listing out and always referring to your top three goals in any aspect of life—the rest is just noise.

Sabio es quien poco habla y mucho calla.

DIRECT TRANSLATION

Wise is the one who speaks little and stays silent often.

MODERN TRANSLATION

Just shut up sometimes.

We're all guilty of wanting to be the first to chime in or break the silence, but the truth is, the more we listen, the more we understand. Listening builds empathy, and we all have something to learn from each other. That, and like our **mamás** would always say: the quieter you are, the more others will talk, giving you the upper hand with the intel you gather. Okay, **Señoras** Spies!

Sabio es quien poco habla y mucho calla. You never know what you might uncover if you just sit back and let others spill the **frijoles**. You can also gather a lot of context from tone and body language, cues that are easy to miss when you're the one yapping like a chihuahua. Embrace the power of shutting up, and you might even reach wise **abuela** status before you hit middle age.

Más sabe el diablo por viejo que por diablo.

DIRECT TRANSLATION

The devil knows more because he is old than because he is the devil.

MODERN TRANSLATION

Wisdom levels up with age.

Our moms often reminded us that, with their years of experience, they knew better than we did. Now that we're in our **señora** era, we finally get it.

The years have aged us and given us a lot more insight than we had in our early twenties. Sure, we'd sell our souls just to drop it to the floor and throw back tequila shots without suffering a two-day hangover, but we'll settle for some liquid collagen and the wisdom that's come with age.

Más sabe el diablo por viejo que por diablo. So the next time your mom offers you unsolicited advice about your diet choices or critiques how you're doing your laundry, take a deep breath and remember: she's not just older; she's wiser. And trust us, you'll be doing the same thing to your kids someday.

Summary for Las Perezosas

In this chapter, we touched on how to be smart in a world full of uncertainty, tested boundaries, and distracting gossip. Here is a summary for **las perezosas**, a condensed version of everything we've covered if you need a quick reference or are just too lazy to read the full thing. Dog-ear this page for quick access to these cute bites of wisdom next time you need to remind a friend—and yourself—how to not be a **pendeja**.

- **Stop ignoring the red flags!** Don't cherry-pick good qualities and overlook bad ones just because it's convenient.

- **Your *amiga* may mean well, but that doesn't mean her advice is worth listening to.** Consider the source before you take it to heart.

- **Not everything needs to be shared on the group chat.** Keep some things close to the chest to preserve your good energy and fortune.

- **The best opportunity is the one you go for.** Don't sit around and wait for the perfect moment to come along; take action on your goals right now.

- **Stay out of other people's drama—you've got your own to worry about.** Think twice before you get involved in matters that don't concern you or share opinions on something you don't know enough about.

- **No matter how many times you repeat yourself, you can't force someone to listen to you.** Some lessons have to be learned the hard way.

- **An ounce of preparation is worth a cubic ton of "I told you so."** Listen to your *mamá's* warnings and stay prepared for anything.

- **Habits will make or break you.** Be organized and maintain healthy habits so you can handle anything life throws your way.

- **Don't get lost in the sauce.** Priorities are key to making shit happen.

- **Sometimes you need to find your ears, not your voice.** When you listen more than talk, you learn to understand others better and communicate beyond your years.

- **Don't sleep on a *viejo's* advice!** The wisdom they've gained through their experience is worth a listen.

Check Your Damn Attitude

Repeat after us: "I am a badass, and I can handle anything life throws at me." Now, let's dive into the power of a positive mindset, because let's face it, sometimes the only thing standing between you and greatness is that little voice in your head that sounds suspiciously like our depressed Tía Rosa after a few too many margaritas.

No se ahogue en un vaso de agua.

DIRECT TRANSLATION

Don't drown in a glass of water.

MODERN TRANSLATION

Dial down the drama, queen!

Abuela always said, "If it won't matter in five years, don't stress for more than five hours." She had a point. In your mind, you might be drowning, but in reality, it's just a splash in a glass.

If even the smallest trigger gives you an anxiety attack, understand that the intensity of your problems is determined only by your mindset. Ghosted by your crush? Maybe they can't handle your spicy self. Flight delayed? Time for a Netflix binge at the airport bar. *¡No se ahogue en un vaso de agua!* Staying level-headed will make life much smoother, so keep your head above water and drama below sea level.

A mal tiempo, buena cara.

DIRECT TRANSLATION

To bad times, good face.

MODERN TRANSLATION

Look up, buttercup.

Life is hard, we get it. You left your laundry in the washer for too long and now everything smells like wet dog. The global pandemic canceled your dream vacation—hell, maybe even your wedding.

¡A mal tiempo, buena cara! You can't control everything, but you can control your reaction. Endlessly venting or scrolling for hours on social media won't pull you out of your funk. When you ditch this victory-versus-defeat mindset, you'll have more time to focus on what you can change, not what you can't.

A caballo regalado no se le mira el colmillo.

DIRECT TRANSLATION

You don't look at the tooth of a gifted horse.

MODERN TRANSLATION

Gratitude over attitude!

Don't be a diva when you receive a gift or favor and it's not perfect or what you expected. When you feel your inner brat emerging, take a moment to find something positive you might've missed.

Your friends got you escape room tickets? Though you can't even solve the mystery of which roommate stole your bag of Takis last week, appreciate it! Your spouse surprised you with a Disney trip during the hottest month of the year? Enjoy it, sweat and all! Your tías bought tacky baby shower decorations? Smile and say **"gracias." A caballo regalado no se le mira el colmillo**. Be grateful for what you get, and the universe might just upgrade you to first-class blessings.

Con hambre, no hay pan duro.

DIRECT TRANSLATION

With hunger, there's no hard bread.

MODERN TRANSLATION

Take it or leave it.

If you're hungry enough, you'll eat whatever's on the table. Same goes for life. Crying about a lack of money, good men, or the ideal body? Sounds like you're not giving it your hundred percent.

Well, **_con hambre, no hay pan duro_**. Stop answering those 3 a.m. "U up?" texts. Quit impulse buying on Amazon and put down the damn margaritas! Not every problem is easy to solve, but if you can reflect on how you might be blocking your own progress, then making a change becomes more manageable. Work with what you've got, and level up from there.

No hay mal que por bien no venga.

DIRECT TRANSLATION

There is no bad that doesn't come with some good.

MODERN TRANSLATION

Find the damn silver lining.

Whether you're going through a breakup, got fired from work, or parted ways with a friend, know that something positive will come from it.

¡No hay mal que por bien no venga! That ex wasn't right for you anyway. Imagine the future custody battles! Losing your job could open new doors (especially ones that pay better). And that friend who couldn't pass the vibe check? Better off without 'em. Even in your darkest times, there's a silver lining, and if you take a moment to reflect and find it, you'll rise from the ashes.

Dios aprieta, pero no ahorca.

DIRECTION TRANSLATION

God squeezes but does not strangle.

MODERN TRANSLATION

Life might choke you, but it won't kill you.

The universe will put you through it! You know what we're talking about: those days, weeks, months, or years when everything seems to go wrong, and it's one piece of bad news after the other. It may feel like there's no way to rid yourself of the storm cloud above your head, but remember, **Dios aprieta, pero no ahorca**.

Believe that you will find that solution to save your business or mortgage. You will survive the trolls on social media. You will make it through those thirty minutes jogging on the treadmill! Because nothing lasts forever, including the moments that feel the most unbearable. As morbid as it sounds, the only problem without a solution is death—and even then, at least you won't have bills to worry about! Remember this saying next time you feel like you just can't catch a break. You've got this, **amor**!

Mugre que no mata, engorda.

DIRECT TRANSLATION

Dirt that doesn't kill makes you fat.

MODERN TRANSLATION

You'll survive.

You are not a delicate flower, and neither were our **mamás**. They lived by the ancient five-second rule—a little dirt (or ants!) on your food wouldn't kill you, and at least it gave you some extra protein.

This applies to life too. Crazy roommate who claims that washing their own dishes is against their religious beliefs? The lease on that godforsaken apartment will end. That crypto scam you got suckered into? You'll make the money back. ***Mugre que no mata, engorda***. Most fuckups won't kill you. They'll teach you how strong you are and make for great stories to tell at parties!

Si a vieja quieres llegar, las cargas has de soltar.

DIRECT TRANSLATION

If you want to grow old, you have to let go of the burdens.

MODERN TRANSLATION

Drop that baggage like it's hot!

Time isn't the only thing that ages you—think constant road rage, binging late-night Taco Bell, or skipping sunscreen on cloudy days (it's still essential!). But the number one thing that takes years off your life? Emotional baggage. Sure, you can chase the fountain of youth with a nip here or a tuck there, but what good is a smooth forehead if you're a bitter **infeliz** on the inside?

Si a vieja quieres llegar, las cargas has de soltar. If you're over thirty and still blaming your parents for your shortcomings, it's time to take accountability. Enough with holding that grudge against your ex-partner! They might have screwed you big-time, but blaming them won't help you move on. So do yourself a favor and let that shit go.

Al que no quiere caldo, se le dan tres tazas.

DIRECT TRANSLATION

Those who don't want soup are given three servings.

MODERN TRANSLATION

Attract, don't repel.

Stop obsessing over what you don't want to happen. It's natural to let your nerves and fears get the best of your imagination. But when these worst-case scenarios become all you think about, you suddenly find them coming true!

Running late for a meeting? Suddenly, your pants get caught in the car door, you forget your wallet, and there's an accident on the road. Worried about messing up your speech at your best friend's wedding? Hello, drunk rambling—meet pity claps from the guests.

Al que no quiere caldo se le dan tres tazas. Next time you start spiraling down that rabbit hole of the undesirable, flip the script. Visualize success instead. It beats non-stop worrying and might just manifest the positive outcome you're hoping for.

Uno no es moneda de veinte para que todos lo quieran.

DIRECT TRANSLATION

You're not a twenty-cent coin for everyone to love you.

MODERN TRANSLATION

You don't need everyone's love.

Let's get over the fact that our ancestors chose a measly twenty-cent coin to compare us to instead of a Benjamin. Anyway, the point is that not everyone is going to like you—and that's okay!

Don't spiral into self-doubt when someone doesn't vibe with you. Most of the time, it's not even about you (unless you puked on their family heirloom rug at their party—that reason might be valid).

Uno no es moneda de veinte para que todos lo quieran. Focus on the people who love you for who you are, flaws and all.

Summary for Las Peresozas

In this chapter, we covered advice on how to keep a strong, confident, and positive mindset when faced with life's bullshit. Our **mamás** didn't have time for pity parties or mental breakdowns—they were too busy being **guerreras**, working hard to make ends meet. So if you're feeling sorry for yourself and need a swift kick to the **culo** to snap back to being your best, finest self, here's your recap.

- **Mindset is everything.** It's not just about putting on a brave face—it's about not letting anything deter you from getting through your battles.

- **Appreciate what comes your way no matter how imperfect.** Practicing gratitude will open doors to more desirable gifts and blessings.

- **Take what's offered and make it work.** If you're really passionate about achieving a goal, you'll take what you can get to keep moving forward.

- **It's not that serious!** Don't be a drama queen over the smallest inconvenience. Keep things in perspective and save your tears for the bigger hurdles.

- **Pity parties are canceled.** Taking a step back to refocus on the pros in any situation, especially the ones that feel like they only have cons, will help you quickly overcome challenging times.

- **You're stronger than you think.** Our ancestors survived wars, famines, and colonization—you can survive a tough week at work or a bad breakup.

- **Turn your pain into power.** Every challenge you face is a chance to learn, grow, and prove your own strength to yourself. Count each setback as a setup for reaching your goals.

- **Don't become bitter as you age.** Aging is inevitable, but you can maintain your youth longer by leaving behind grudges and tossing out emotional baggage.

- **Keep that worst-case scenario out of your head!** Focus on what you want to attract—not repel—and the universe will take note!

- **You can't please everyone, so why try so hard?** Get over it, be confident in yourself, and concentrate on those who love you for who you are.

Guard It, Don't Lock It

Ah, love. It's like a spicy salsa dance—exhilarating, passionate, and sometimes painful when your partner steps on your toes. But fear not, because in this chapter, we'll explore the wisdom of our ancestors on navigating the wild world of not just *amor*, but all types of relationships. And trust us, they knew a thing or two about how to keep the flame burning without getting burned themselves.

Dime con quién andas, y te diré quién eres.

DIRECT TRANSLATION

Tell me who you walk with, and I'll tell you who you are.

MODERN TRANSLATION

If your friends are trash, so are you.

Our Latina mothers always seemed to have a sixth sense when it came to judging our friends or partners. Despite not knowing much about them, they were always quick to call out red flags. Yet, this **bruja** intuition always proved true once these relationships ultimately failed. As adults, we've developed our own instincts when it comes to people we choose to have around us.

Dime con quién andas, y te diré quién eres.

You're supposedly a reflection of the five people you spend the most time with—are they smart, caring, and upbeat? If so, chances are, so are you. If they're a bunch of complainers and slackers, it's time for a squad overhaul. Keeping the right company is as important as working on yourself, so choose wisely, unless you want to be the trash friend everyone warns their kids about.

Ojos que no ven, corazón que no siente.

DIRECT TRANSLATION
Eyes that don't see, heart that doesn't feel.

MODERN TRANSLATION
Out of sight, out of mind.

Moving on demands action, not just desire.

Take it from our friend, Claudia, who stalked her ex on social media months after they broke up; or our cousin, Kevin, who kept a box of ex-memorabilia, like movie tickets and hotel room keys. These visual reminders only kept them stuck in the past. The day Claudia unfollowed her ex and Kevin threw out his heartbreaking box of junk was the day they finally felt capable of moving on.

Ojos que no ven, corazón que no siente. Block, unfollow, delete, build a bonfire in your backyard with those happy-couple photos as kindling— whatever it takes to put them out of sight and out of mind. As you clear out the old, you make room for new joys, memories, and love.

perro que no se conoce, no se le coje la cola.

DIRECT TRANSLATION

Don't know the dog, don't grab its tail.

MODERN TRANSLATION

Don't get too friendly too quickly.

Even if someone seems great at first, proceed with caution! Our **mamás** taught us that true character emerges over time. That shiny new coworker or flame might seem perfect, but rush in without testing the relationship and you risk being trapped or hurt.

So take it slow. Observe how new friends or partners handle responsibilities, stress, and disagreements. Engage in different types of activities that will start to peel back their layers.

Remember, **perro que no se conoce, no se le coje la cola**. Keep your eyes open and your judgment pending until you really get to know someone. Don't let your life turn into a **telenovela**, one minute feeling like you know everyone's intentions, the next *bam!* You're shocked to find out it was the evil twin who put the neighbor in a coma all along.

A donde el corazón se inclina, el pie camina.

DIRECT TRANSLATION
Where the heart is inclined, the foot walks.

MODERN TRANSLATION
Your heart is your intuition.

Our families always told us to listen to that inner voice, especially when it comes to love. Think of this voice as the backseat driver of your life. Sometimes annoying, sure, but often right about the direction you should be taking.

Imagine you had to choose between two job offers: one that paid more but felt about as exciting as watching paint dry, and another that set your soul on fire but barely covered your rent. Your brain said, "Take the money and run," but your heart said, "Follow your dreams, even if you have to eat ramen for a year." Which would you choose? We'd bet you'd take a leap of faith and trust your instincts. And while it's not always easy, you'll never regret dancing to the beat of your own **corazón**.

A donde el corazón se inclina, el pie camina. Wherever your heart throws a **fiesta**, make sure your feet are ready to salsa dance right along with it, even if they occasionally step on a few toes!

Cuentas claras y chocolate espeso.

DIRECT TRANSLATION
Clear accounts and thick chocolate.

MODERN TRANSLATION
Don't sugarcoat your boundaries!

Let's be honest: nobody likes watery hot chocolate or murky relationships! Whether you're ordering from a server or setting dating deal-breakers, establishing clear expectations is key. Don't be like our cousin Danny, who lent his brother $5,000 and said, "Pay me back whenever," only to find him hitting up the casino while still indebted. Clarify if and when you expect your favor returned. Confused about your situationship? Bring up the label question before catching major feelings so everyone's on the same page.

Cuentas claras y chocolate espeso isn't just about avoiding the bitter taste of disappointment; it's about savoring the sweet success of well-managed relationships. So keep those expectations clear, and all your interactions will be as smooth and satisfying as a deliciously creamy *chocolate espeso*.

A la sombra de los buenos, viven los malos sin freno.

DIRECT TRANSLATION
Under the shadow of the good, the bad live without brakes.

MODERN TRANSLATION
Trust with a grain of salt.

Haters are everywhere, even hidden among those closest to you. Like our **mamás** always said, **"Guarda tus secretos bien guardados."** You never know who's smiling with you but not for you. Even Jesus was betrayed by his boy Judas.

A la sombra de los buenos, viven los malos sin freno. Balance your openness with a healthy dose of caution. Share enough to create real connections, but keep your most precious details safe. Preserving your peace sometimes means not letting everyone know what treasure is buried.

A rey muerto, rey puesto.

DIRECT TRANSLATION
A dead king, a king in his place.

MODERN TRANSLATION
No one's that special.

Nobody is indispensable. We often linger in situations longer than we should, whether it's staying at a job just because they "need" us or keeping a clingy relationship to avoid hurting feelings. But you're not anyone's superhero. They'll figure it out without you.

In addition, the fear that you might not find—or perhaps don't deserve—something or someone better can keep you stuck.

A rey muerto, rey puesto: One king falls, another is crowned. Even when you feel devastated by loss, remember that life is full of changes and fresh starts. Don't let fear or guilt keep you from your next special connection or opportunity.

Donde come uno, comen dos.

DIRECT TRANSLATION
Where one eats, two eat.

MODERN TRANSLATION
There's always room for more.

Seeing our **mamás** stretch that last bit of **carne asada** to feed the unexpected visit from our **tíos** taught us there's always room for one more. Those ladies were the queens of "make it work" long before it was a hashtag.

But it's not just about food; it's about widening our hearts too. It's like that small dinner turned full-blown fiesta when too many plus-ones arrive. Despite the chaos, the fun and laughter often make a home feel like a grand hall.

Donde come uno, comen dos. In friendships, love, and everyday interactions, there's always space for extra kindness—even half of your tortilla.

Le cuento el milagro pero no el santo.

DIRECT TRANSLATION

I'll tell you the miracle but not the saint.

MODERN TRANSLATION

Don't be a big mouth.

We all love a good gossip sesh, spilling the tea with the girls over a bottle (or three) of wine. But not everything belongs on your social pages.

Le cuento el milagro pero no el santo. Though it's fun to be a **chismosa**, being a blabbermouth is a surefire way to lose respect. No one will confide in you if you can't keep your mouth shut because they'll wonder what you're saying about them behind their backs. Be selective about what you share to maintain trust with your people. While it's good to be open and transparent, oversharing others' lives, or your own, can bite you in the ass.

Téngale miedo al agua mansa, que de la turbulenta me salvo yo.

DIRECT TRANSLATION
Be afraid of the calm water because I am saved from the turbulent one.

MODERN TRANSLATION
Expect the unexpected.

With life's twists and turns, even quiet moments can often hide the biggest surprises. When things seem suspiciously smooth, <u>stay alert</u>! Keep your side-eye sharp and your BS detector fully charged. That quiet, minimalist roommate who's barely added furniture to their room? They might be getting ready to break the lease without telling you. Fewer emails in your inbox so "you're not being overworked"? Watch out—could be a sign of getting fired soon!

Téngale miedo al agua mansa, que de la turbulenta me salvo yo. Navigating life isn't just about enjoying the calm; it's about being prepared for when the waters suddenly chop. Don't always expect the worst, but don't be blindsided either.

Cuando el muerto tiene quien lo cargue, se pone pesado.

DIRECT TRANSLATION

When the dead find someone to carry them, they get heavier.

MODERN TRANSLATION

Beware the leeches around you.

Abuela always warned us: People will test your limits as far as you allow. It's human nature to push boundaries, but without a backbone, you'll be trampled like roadkill. Know when to draw the line, and be brave enough to say no to those who demand too much—whether it's money, favors, or your precious time.

Cuando el muerto tiene quien lo cargue, se pone pesado. When someone knows you'll carry them, they might just make themselves heavier. Don't risk your own job covering for a coworker's endless personal emergencies. Think twice about moving in with the partner who wants to share space but not expenses. Give the support you expect and set clear boundaries or you'll easily get taken advantage of! Helping others doesn't mean you have to kill yourself in the process.

Summary for Las Peresozas

In this chapter, we channeled love and relationship lessons our **mamás** passed down to us. They knew the secret to thriving started with self-love sprinkled with mutual respect and clear boundaries.

Here's your quick recap of how to navigate the challenges of modern romance and adult friendships like a **chingona**.

- **You are the company you keep.** Surround yourself with people who share your morals, goals, and aspirations.

- **When it's time to move on, actually move on.** When relationships run their course, cut the cord completely. Any lingering reminders can trap you in the past.

- **Don't trust people right away.** Ease into new relationships with caution, letting time peel back the layers of those charming new faces.

- **Your heart is your intuition.** When it comes to love and relationships, learn to pay attention to your gut feeling. It's usually not wrong.

- **Set your boundaries and set people straight!** Be clear and thorough with your intentions, boundaries, and expectations. Stand firm in what you want and believe in.

- **Watch your back.** Make sure you are selective and careful with the information you share and the trust you offer.

- **Everyone is replaceable.** Remember, no one is too important to be irreplaceable, from your barista to your beau.

- **There's always space at the table.** Even when resources seem limited, there's always a way to share and support others.

- **STFU.** Oversharing your life or others' lives can kill trust and intimacy.

- **Be ready for anything from anyone.** Never feel so secure in a relationship that you blindly trust someone. There should always be a bit of skepticism and readiness for something to go awry.

- **You do not have to be everyone's hero.** You do you, and let others manage their own drama. You can only control your actions and reactions, so make them count.

Gotta Love That Bitch

Do you believe in destiny? How about karma? Well, our ancestors sure did, and they had a lot to say about how the universe rewards you. In this chapter, we'll explore the age-old notion of "what goes around comes around," discovering how to navigate life's twists with humility and a bit of divine assistance.

A cada marrano le llega su sábado.

DIRECT TRANSLATION

Every pig gets his Saturday.

MODERN TRANSLATION

Let Karma do her thing.

Karma's a bitch, but she seems to run on Latino time. Don't let a thirst for revenge make you do something that you'll regret, like rubbing jalapeño all over your cheating ex's underwear. More often than not, seeking revenge or holding on to negativity does not make us feel better and may mess with our own fortune.

A cada marrano le llega su sábado. In due time, that asshole will get what's coming to them. That prick of a manager treating everyone else like shit? She'll probably get fired and end up involved with some pyramid scheme on Facebook. And that dude who cut you off on the highway will have his insurance premiums skyrocket when he rams into a mailbox. Trust that karma will catch up to them without you playing God. Focus on being your best self, and let the universe handle the rest.

Cada loco con su tema.

DIRECT TRANSLATION

Each crazy person with their theme.

MODERN TRANSLATION

Focus on you, boo.

There will always be people who do things so differently than you that you can't help but judge. Your friend sexting her married boss, your sister packing her kids' backpacks with "good-luck crystals," your cousin redoing his kitchen but having no money to fill his fridge. Well, ¡**cada loco con su tema**!

Kill the urge to get involved in matters that don't concern you and, instead, focus on your own possibly questionable decisions. Don't get distracted from your own main-character plot. You're better off saving your energy for your own challenges, like learning to cook more than just **arroz y huevos** or curbing your Candy Crush obsession.

Una buena acción es la mejor oración.

DIRECT TRANSLATION
A good deed is the best prayer.

MODERN TRANSLATION
Good deeds bring good vibes.

The universe has a way of tossing back what you throw at it. If you're out there being spiteful and selfish, brace yourself for a cosmic boomerang.

Feeling underappreciated at work or stuck in a rut? Next time you're waiting for things to turn around, ask yourself how you can help make someone's day a little less miserable. Show gratitude to a stressed-out coworker, or give a meal to a homeless person. Because **una buena acción es la mejor oración**. Though we're all struggling, there's always someone who could use a little more help. Rise above your own adversity by doing good and see how it might just come back to bite you . . . in a good way.

Al caído no se le cae.

DIRECT TRANSLATION
Don't fall on the fallen.

MODERN TRANSLATION
Don't shit on people when they're down.

You never know what someone's going through, so always lead with compassion. Don't be so self-absorbed that you can't empathize with others. Karma doesn't miss anyone, especially those who kick others when they're down.

Want to go off on a rude clerk at the DMV or joke about someone's terrible new haircut after they've just been dumped? *¡Al caído no se le cae!* Bite your tongue and hold back any impulsive actions that could make their day even worse. Offer grace and empathy, even if they're moving slower than your **abuelo** at a buffet. Don't add to their plate, especially if it's already full of pain.

A lo hecho, pecho.

DIRECT TRANSLATION
To what's done, chest.

MODERN TRANSLATION
What happened happened!

Our moms taught us that **lo bueno y lo malo** come in waves, and dwelling on the past gets you nowhere. The past is the past, and all you can do is learn from it and try to do better next time. Don't be that **pendeja** stuck living in it.

Sure, you can dwell on the time you spent watching *Tiger King* during quarantine instead of learning how to bake sourdough bread like everyone else on Instagram. Or you can stalk your seventh-grade boyfriend's wedding and dream about "what-ifs." But ¡**a lo hecho, pecho**! Shift your mindset, accept that what happened was part of your journey, and move on. Embrace the plot twists and look up at the next exciting chapter!

El que mucho escoge, lo peor se lleva.

DIRECT TRANSLATION

The pickiest person chooses the worst.

MODERN TRANSLATION

Don't wait around for perfection.

Perfection doesn't exist, and if you wait too long, you might end up with the last crusty **pastelito** at the **panadería**. Holding out for the perfect partner, house, or job can lead to settling for less as options dwindle over time.

Waiting for that perfect moment to start the side hustle? Hoping for your dream home to magically fit your budget? **El que mucho escoge, lo peor se lleva**. Keep waiting, **corazón**, and you might let existing chances slip by.

It's good to be selective, but don't dismiss opportunities just because they don't fit your specific vision. Take a chance on the less-than-perfect maybes; they might just surprise you.

Si quieres el perro, acepta las pulgas.

DIRECT TRANSLATION

If you want the dog, accept the fleas.

MODERN TRANSLATION

Accept the consequences of your actions.

No one else is to blame for the outcome of the choices you make. Your actions have consequences, both good and bad. At a certain point, you have to own your shit!

This saying usually comes up when someone is about to make a questionable choice. Oh, you want to settle down but are still thinking of dating the rebel with the motorcycle? Planning a night of barhopping but taking your car instead of ride-sharing? Eyeing a purebred Frenchie when you're struggling to make rent this month? Well, **si quieres el perro, acepta las pulgas**. Brace yourself for potential drawbacks—it's as simple as that.

Tanto va el cántaro al agua que al fin se rompe.

DIRECT TRANSLATION

The pitcher goes so far into the water that it finally breaks.

MODERN TRANSLATION

Screw around and eventually you'll get screwed.

It's been said that insanity is doing the same thing repeatedly, expecting different outcomes—and yet, here we are, often stuck on replay. Like when you pull three all-nighters in one week, then have the audacity to wonder why you can't stay awake during your Thursday meetings. Venturing into risky situations over and over again will inevitably lead to shit hitting the fan. And you're the fan.

Rekindling flames with that toxic ex who never cared to drop you off at home, stirring up drama at work, or consistently overdoing it on the weekends? **¡*Tanto va el cántaro al agua que al fin se rompe!*** Eventually, these repeated actions lead to predictable outcomes—another painful breakup, workplace trouble, or just plain burnout.

So stop screwing around. Making these kinds of decisions habitual will eventually pull you into a dangerous current you can't escape from.

Uno no valora lo que tiene hasta que lo pierde.

DIRECT TRANSLATION

You don't value what you have till you lose it.

MODERN TRANSLATION

You never know what you've got till it's gone!

We often overlook the daily gifts in our lives—our health, family, jobs, or friends—fixating on what goes wrong instead of what's right. Think about it: When was the last time you paused to appreciate these **bendiciones?** Karma doesn't play nice; take something for granted, and one day, it might just be gone.

Next time you're counting your blessings, ask yourself: What would you tell your loved ones if today were your last chance? Stop waiting and text them now.

Uno no valora lo que tiene hasta que lo pierde. Don't just value your life's gifts—shout out your thanks. Whether it's those blessed earrings from Mom or a storm that saved you from a dreadful event, showing gratitude can change your world for the better. Don't believe us? Try it—see what happens.

Nadie te quita lo que está pa' ti.

DIRECT TRANSLATION

No one takes away what's meant for you.

MODERN TRANSLATION

What's meant for you will find you.

Whenever things didn't go as we planned, our **mamás** would remind us of this saying, which always made things feel instantly more bearable. It may not feel the same way for you at the moment. especially when defeat has you losing count of how many margaritas you had last night. But when you start to think of the blessings to come, rather than what you failed to gain, you open your mind to grander possibilities.

You got a rejection email for that role you had three interviews for? You didn't get approved for that ideal apartment with the balcony? It's okay! **Nadie te quita lo que está pa' ti.** Zoom out to the bigger picture and think—a better job or apartment is waiting for you right around the corner.

Because what's meant for you will show up when it's supposed to.

Summary for Las Peresozas

In this chapter, we covered navigating life's roller coasters with cosmic finesse. Embrace the chaos, and accept that some things are out of your control, so best let the universe do its thing at times.

Here's a summary on how you can lean into your own potential and trust the unseen forces, like faith and karma, to guide you.

- **You have your own things to focus on.** Don't be criticizing others for doing things differently than you. You have your own flaws and decisions to worry about.

- **Everyone gets what they deserve.** It's not your job to balance the karmic scales for others. Feelings of revenge or pettiness will only mess with your own fortune.

- **Help others and the universe will help you.** Remember, when you're weighed down by problems, you're not alone. Acting selflessly can tilt karma in your favor.

- **Don't be an asshole.** Dial back the main-character energy to consider others' feelings before you say or do something that may add to their misery.

- **Onto the next chapter!** Don't dwell on the past—it's out of your control. Focus on your reaction and how you move forward.

- **Perfect doesn't exist.** Don't be so picky with life choices that you wait till it's too late and end up settling for the worst pick of the pack.

- **Play stupid games, win stupid prizes!** If you're going to make questionable choices, be prepared for the inevitable consequences.

- **Repeat offenders get a harder sentence.** Commit the same mistakes or repeat negative habits, and it's only a matter of time before you deal with the repercussions.

- **Appreciate it before you lose it.** Show gratitude for what's in your life, because you never know when it won't be there anymore.

- **Don't cry over that job you didn't get.** Trust the process and know you will get what you deserve.

Ain't for Slackers

Raised by women who worked their asses off and could negotiate like they were bargaining at a *mercado*, we learned to stand up for ourselves, especially in our careers. This chapter is all about channeling that same hustle mindset to put in the work, curate your inner circle, and not let any *pendejos* get in the way.

A Dios rogando y con el mazo dando.

DIRECTION TRANSLATION

Begging to God and hitting with the hammer.

MODERN TRANSLATION

Pray for it—but work for it too.

Spirituality and hope have their place, but waiting for divine intervention won't cut it when it comes to achieving your goals. Even if you're grinding away on seemingly unattainable milestones, there's always opportunity for a new approach to create better outcomes.

Not seeing results despite hitting the gym religiously? Maybe those late-night **taquitos** are sabotaging your body goals! Slaving away at your business but seeing no progress? Time to pivot strategies! The best goals require patience and consistent effort.

So, before you surrender to a life of sweatpants and couch potato status, remember: **A Dios rogando y con el mazo dando**. Combine faith—both in yourself and the universe—with hard work and strategic planning, and you've got a **chingón** formula for success.

El que no llora, no mama.

DIRECT TRANSLATION

The baby who doesn't cry does not suckle.

MODERN TRANSLATION

If you don't ask, the answer is always no.

Sometimes we don't ask for what we want out of fear of rejection or inconveniencing others. But without communication, we'll spend our lives yearning for what we think we can't have. And we're not talking about entitled Karens—if there's something that will bring you inner peace or advance you toward your goals, go for it!

El que no llora, no mama. If you don't ask, you won't receive. It could be as simple as asking your seatmate to turn down their loud-ass music during your morning train commute, or as important as requesting a well-deserved raise at work. Channel your inner Sofía Vergara and speak up! That confidence can be yours. You'd be surprised how often you'll succeed just by voicing your desires.

A quien madruga, Dios le ayuda.

DIRECT TRANSLATION

Whoever rises early, God helps.

MODERN TRANSLATION

The earlier, the better—even if you hit the snooze button a couple of times.

Being late is a trash habit! Unless you're headed to a Latino party (where everyone knows to roll up at least two hours late), tardiness is just plain rude. Drop the excuses and arrive on time to avoid being seen as unreliable and missing out on opportunities.

Stop hitting snooze and running around like a **pollo loco** before work every morning. Don't ignore that check-engine light unless you want to be stuck on the side of the road with a busted vehicle. Remember, **a quien madruga, Dios lo ayuda**. Do things early or on time, and watch life go much more smoothly. Plus, you'll avoid that frantic anxiety you get running late. You know the feeling!

Quien con el lobo se junta, a aullar aprende.

DIRECT TRANSLATION

Who joins the wolf learns to howl.

MODERN TRANSLATION

Hang out with winners, and you'll learn how to win.

The company we keep strongly influences our attitudes, beliefs, and behaviors. Just look at successful duos like Sonia Sotomayor and Barack Obama, Bill Gates and Warren Buffett, or Selena Gomez and Taylor Swift. Surround yourself with others who have similar goals and admirable traits, and you'll be on the path to success. Stick with a crew that lacks the same values, and you'll hinder your journey.

Quien con el lobo se junta, a aullar aprende. It's all about who you run with. Though it may seem daunting, seeking and fostering these connections is crucial for paving your path to success. Build your wolf pack of trusted friends who support you as much as you support them, and you'll be fucking unstoppable.

El que tiene tienda, que la atienda.

DIRECT TRANSLATION

Whoever has a store should attend it.

MODERN TRANSLATION

You made your bed, now lie in it (even if it's full of crumbs and regret).

Stop playing the blame game! Your love life is a hot mess? That's on you, boo. Career going nowhere? How much effort are you really putting in? Toxic friends? Time for an upgrade. Hold yourself accountable, even when it's easiest to play the victim. The only way to get ahead is to own your choices and their consequences.

El que tiene tienda, que la atienda. While supportive friends and family are great, you are the only one who can fix your life. You may think you're the star of your own drama series, but true power comes when you realize you're actually the director. Take charge and own your story, even if it means cleaning up a few metaphorical (or literal) messes along the way.

Usted oyo campanas y no sabe donde.

DIRECT TRANSLATION

You heard bells and don't know from where.

MODERN TRANSLATION

Fact-check yourself before you wreck yourself.

Before voicing your opinion or speaking some "truth," make sure you've got your facts straight. In a world where everyone's got something to say, yapping without knowledge makes you look like an unreliable **imbécil**.

Usted oyó campanas y no sabe dónde. Are you sure Samantha missed the deadline, or are you assuming? Did you research the benefits of high cheese consumption, or are you just making excuses for downing all that queso? If you're not sure about something, admit it. In business as in life, humility beats lazy guesses any day. So, if you're going to talk, be ready to back up your words (maybe with a quick Google search under the table).

Subir como palmera para caer como coco.

DIRECT TRANSLATION

Rise like a palm tree to fall like a coconut.

MODERN TRANSLATION

Quick rise, swift demise!

We all love an overnight success story: the single mom turned viral star, the once homeless lottery winner. But lasting success takes time. Quickly won fortune, whirlwind romances, and lucky streaks often plummet because they're unsustainable, rarely built on lessons learned or hard work materialized. Take it from people who know: the faster you rise, the harder you fall. Without a solid foundation, what you have now won't last.

You don't want to **subir como palmera para caer como coco.** Learn from each "failure" or lesson during your journey, no matter how painstaking or slow it feels. In time, experience will protect you from falling like a coconut from a palm tree. (And trust, that shit will hurt.)

Las palabras sueltas se las lleva el viento.

DIRECT TRANSLATION

Loose words are carried away by the wind.

MODERN TRANSLATION

Put your money where your mouth is.

Our **mamás** didn't have **pelos en la lengua**—they'd call us out for not following through on promises, like fixing that ancient printer we said we'd get to **ahorita**. The value they placed on commitment taught us to stay dedicated to bigger things in life—like executing a real-life product instead of just dwelling on start-up ideas, or supporting a nonprofit rather than blabbing about our love for a cause.

Las palabras sueltas se las lleva el viento. Actions always speak louder than words, so don't be all talk and no action. Show up and prove you're not just a flaky **pendeja** who can't be counted on. Prove your dedication and reliability, or brace yourself for those "I'm not angry, just disappointed" looks.

Tantas manos en un plato, pronto se acaba el caldo.

DIRECT TRANSLATION

So many hands on a plate, the broth soon runs out.

MODERN TRANSLATION

You do you, boo (even if it means telling everyone else to mind their damn business).

Picture ten **tías** in the kitchen, arguing over a simple pot of **caldo**. They're bumping into each other, arguing over how much salt or water to add. It's a mess! Too many cooks spoil the broth, and too many opinions can cloud your own judgment. Don't let the noise drown out your voice.

¡Tantas manos en un plato, pronto se acaba el caldo! You don't need your hairstylist weighing in on your parenting style, nor your neighbor advising you on career moves. Ultimately, you're the one who has to live with your choices—not the peanut gallery. So do what feels right to you, even if your ten **tías** say differently.

Como dijo una loca, cuando toca, toca.

DIRECT TRANSLATION

As a crazy woman said, when it's time, it's time.

MODERN TRANSLATION

Get out of bed and just do the damn thing
(even if it means putting on real pants).

Just get it done! Even if it's not perfect. It's easy to procrastinate and get caught up mulling over options before taking action, but you know this only adds to the anxiety of unfinished tasks.

Como dijo una loca, cuando toca, toca. Don't dwell on starting that book you've been talking about for years. Stop delaying the assembly of that IKEA furniture set. At some point, you've got to stop making excuses and start making moves; otherwise, you're just hindering your goals. So talk it out with a friend, research, meditate, burn some **palo santo**—whatever gets you in the zone. The only thing worse than doing something imperfectly is not doing it at all.

Summary for Las Peresozas

If you want to be a boss and make that **dinero**, you've got to *work*. Here are some reminders to keep in your back pocket when motivation is low and inspiration feels harder to come by.

- **Faith and hope only go as far as your own hustle.** Wishing won't pay the bills, so get out of bed and start putting in the work.

- **Ask and you shall receive.** You have to speak up for what you want, or risk never getting it.

- **Showing up late is not a good look, even for Latinas.** You better be on time and ready to shine if you want to make a good impression.

- **You are the company you keep, so choose your squad wisely.** Let go of those who hold you back, and surround yourself with those who lift you up.

- **Playing the victim gets old quick.** Take responsibility for your own life, and stop blaming the world for your problems.

- **Get all your facts straight before yapping.** Don't be like the ***pendeja*** who runs her mouth without knowing what she's talking about. Do your research or keep your mouth shut!

- **Sustainable success doesn't happen overnight, no matter what TikTok says.** Be prepared to put in the time and grind if you want lasting successful results.

- **Actions over words.** Don't just talk; show up and prove your commitment, or risk being seen as unreliable.

- **Don't let the noise drown out your own voice.** Everyone's got opinions, but that doesn't mean you've got to listen to them.

- **Just fucking do it!** Excuses only add to the anxiety, so work toward starting any progress rather than blatantly procrastinating.

Live with the Confidence of a Colombian Woman

Growing up in a household full of confident Colombian women, we learned that Latinas are fierce warriors wrapped in beauty. They know they deserve nothing but the best, and who can blame them? Harness that same confidence in your everyday life to conquer your goals and welcome more blessings. This chapter's all about building resilience and self-respect, so no obstacle can shake you.

Mejor sola que mal acompañada.

DIRECT TRANSLATION
Better alone than in bad company.

MODERN TRANSLATION
Don't let anyone mess with your peace.

This saying was drilled into us Latinas early on, probably because our mothers dealt with too many **machistas**. But, it's not just them—anyone disrupting your peace does not deserve your time or energy! Sure, you might tolerate a friend's BS, but if they're constantly flaking or making out with your crushes, <u>drop that bitch</u> like a bad habit.

As for those terrifying solo moments? **¡Mejor sola que mal acompañada!** Better to be alone than with, say, creepy Jonathan from HR who laughs at his own jokes. Embrace your independent moments, and take time to reflect on who deserves the privilege of your badass presence.

Antes son mis dientes que mis parientes.

DIRECT TRANSLATION

First my teeth, then my parents.

MODERN TRANSLATION

First me, then everyone else.

Prioritizing yourself isn't selfish. It's essential. When you adopt airplane rules and secure your own mask first, you're best equipped to help others without the risk of suffocation (a.k.a. burnout). This may bring guilt, especially with family, but how effective can you really be running on empty?

Antes son mis dientes que mis parientes. Saying no to Sunday brunch plans because you need to recharge? Valid. Taking time for your side hustle, the gym, or a damn walk? True relationships will understand those commitments to yourself—and everyone else can kick rocks.

You can't pour from an empty cup, so fill yours up before worrying about anyone else's.

Haz bien y no mires a quién.

DIRECT TRANSLATION
Do good and don't look at whom.

MODERN TRANSLATION
Stop comparing yourself to others.

"Wow, this account posts three times a day and so many of their videos go viral! I'm a social media failure."

"Look at Marissa—we're the same age and she's already married with a house and two kids! I'm gonna be alone and broke forever."

Sound familiar? Stop stressin', boo. While you're comparing yourself to others, someone else is probably doing the same to you.

Haz bien y no mires a quién. Focus on you, ***amor***. Use others' success as motivation, not a measuring stick. Are you even chasing the same goals? Appreciate how far you've come and keep on hustling. Comparison is the thief of joy (and the cousin of ***pendejadas***). The only person you're truly competing with is yourself.

¡Ponte a limpiar!

DIRECT TRANSLATION
Get to cleaning!

MODERN TRANSLATION
Don't be a dirty bitch.

Our moms would've whooped our asses if our rooms weren't spotless. As one of the best habits we ever developed, being tidy taught us that a clean home isn't just about appearances—it's self-care, inside and out.

Skin breaking out or allergies acting up? ***¡Ponte a limpiar!*** A dusty house means germs galore, wreaking havoc on your skin and immune system. Also, let's be real: When was the last time you washed your bedsheets? Exactly.

Can't focus or feel stressed out? ***¡Ponte a limpiar!*** Clutter = a cluttered mind. Tidy up and watch your productivity soar.

Keep a weekly cleaning schedule (yes, *weekly*) and your body, mind, and soul will thank you. Plus, your place will be booty-call approved. You're welcome.

Respeto llama respeto.

DIRECT TRANSLATION

Respect calls respect.

MODERN TRANSLATION

Respect me, I'll respect you.

Let's be clear, we're not saying you should smack down any **pendeja** who crosses you. That's how you end up with one phone call and a cellmate with face tattoos. But you don't have to take disrespect lying down.

Respeto llama respeto. Real respect is mutual and earned, not inherited. Consider this next time you're tempted to rudely clap back at Mom's annoying comment or silently accept your boss calling you a fuckup on a team call. Speak up but do so respectfully. You teach people how to treat you by what you allow.

Bottom line: don't be a jerk, but don't let jerks walk all over you either. Treat others with respect and demand the same in return. That's how you show the world you're a boss—not a doormat.

No te acomodes más que un desvelado.

DIRECT TRANSLATION

Don't flop around more than a restless sleeper.

MODERN TRANSLATION

Stick to your damn word.

In a world full of endless choices, indecision can leave us stuck—like scrolling through Netflix for hours without ever committing. But flip-flopping on bigger life choices only make things worse.

No te acomodes más que un desvelado. Don't bounce between fad diets and exercise routines without giving them a real shot. And don't give up on your dream career after a few bumps in the road. Sticking to your word shows discipline, reliability, and—most importantly—that you are showing up for yourself. Remember, strong women stay true and see it through!

No se nace caballero; hay que saber serlo.

DIRECT TRANSLATION

You're not born a gentleman; you have to learn to be one.

MODERN TRANSLATION

Becoming a badass takes work, honey.

Admirable qualities—like courtesy, honor, and the ability to stay optimistic with all the **mierda** happening in this world—aren't innate. You have to actively develop these traits over time.

No se nace caballero; hay que saber serlo. Being a true gentleman (or lady) requires more than just good manners—it takes education and practice. Likewise, you may be a natural leader, but you need experience to be an effective manager. Terrified of public speaking? With practice, you could be the next Tony Robbins. Nurturing your strengths and working on your weaknesses will help you evolve into the best version of yourself— one that would make your **abuela** proud.

No le pongas tanta crema a tus tacos.

DIRECT TRANSLATION
Don't put so much cream on your tacos.

MODERN TRANSLATION
You ain't all that!

This saying isn't meant to bring you down but to keep you humble. It's not cute to think you're better than everyone else or to constantly talk about yourself—*ugh*.

No le pongas tanta crema a tus tacos. Who are you to demand your partner have a perfect credit score? Does knowing Drake's hairstylist's sister's dog-sitter make you important? Value your worth, but check your attitude. No need to drop names or brag about yourself and your expectations. Vanity and superiority will only attract fake friends and repel genuine connections. Take a break from yourself and let someone else have the spotlight for once.

Cuando eí rio suena, piedras trae.

DIRECT TRANSLATION

When the river sounds, it brings rocks.

MODERN TRANSLATION

If it sounds like it, that's what it is.

Behind every perception, there's usually a hint of truth. Just like a running river suggests rocks beneath the surface, people and situations often reveal clues about their true nature. Pay attention to those red flags—like how someone speaks, reacts, or just the vibe they give off.

VIP tickets to a Bad Bunny concert for only $200? Your man knows the season of your shoes but swears he's straighter than a ruler? Mmmm, ***cuando el río suena, piedras trae***. Chances are, something's up! Trust your gut, even if it seems like paranoia or fear. That little voice in your head will help you avoid scams, toxic friends, and even bad business. Stay vigilant, and don't let anyone take you for a ***pendeja.***

El sol sale para todos.

DIRECT TRANSLATION

The sun comes out for all.

MODERN TRANSLATION

Everyone has the right to a good life.

If our **abuela** could move to a new country to make a life for herself without knowing the language and with nothing but her three kids and the clothes on their backs, *you* can handle what life throws your way.

El sol sale para todos—"the sun shines on us all." Everyone has bad days, and though our obstacles and privileges may vary, we each have the power to turn our lives around to work toward a brighter future. Focus on your strengths and how far you've come. And never forget that you have just as much right as anyone else to accomplish anything you want in this life!

Summary for Las Perezosas

As we come to the end, these final sayings will help you stay true to yourself and maintain the confidence you deserve to accomplish **lo que sea**. Here's a recap of the lessons to guide you towards more clarity, inner peace, and self-**amor**.

- **Being solo is sometimes the best option.** Let go of the **tóxicos** that bring you down and enjoy your own company.

- **It's you before anyone else!** Schedule time to focus on your own goals and self-care, rather than always being everyone's go-to.

- **Staring at your competition will only turn you into a limón: sour and green with envy.** Focus on your own path rather than feeling like you're racing against others.

- **If your room is gross, so are you.** Clean your room, clear your headspace.

- **Respect is a two-way street.** You're a grown-ass adult that should treat others with respect, and expect nothing less in return.

- **You're not an *arepa*, so don't flip back and forth on your choices.** Make decisions that reflect your values so you're confident enough to stay true to them.

- **No one is born the superstar they eventually become.** It takes consistent work on yourself to build the version of you that will accomplish your kick-ass goals.

- **It's not cute to be your own hype person.** Being confident is one thing. But real self-assurance is knowing you're all that without having to tell the world every five minutes.

- **Trust that little voice that's picking up the not-so-obvious.** Things may appear one way, but many other indicators could tell you if something is worth it or total bullshit.

- **Your future is right there, and there are no excuses to not reach for it.** We all have the ability to go for what we want in life.

Conclusion

And that's a wrap! If you've made it this far, you're officially armed and dangerous, equipped with wisdom sharp enough to slice through any of life's **pendejadas.** We hope you've laughed, maybe shed a tear (hey, no judgment here), and found a new appreciation for the no-nonsense, fierce love that our Latina matriarchs have passed down through generations.

We hope these pages have shown you that life doesn't have to be a series of unfortunate events unless you let it. Every stumble and every face-palm moment is just another chance to stand up stronger and be more **valiente** than before. Remember, every **por pendeja** moment could be a **por poderosa** opportunity in disguise.

So here's to the hustles, the setbacks, and everything in between. Keep this book close to remind you of your desires and your power. And when you see a friend facing her own battles, pass it along their way. It's like sharing a secret weapon that helps you both laugh off the rough patches and come out swinging. Always step boldly, laugh loudly, and never forget: you're not just surviving; you're thriving, just as the universe intended. Thank you for joining us on this tough-love journey. Now, go out there, spread the wisdom, and show the world what it means to be powerful, passionate, and absolutely not a ***pendeja.***

Glossary

a - to

abuela - grandmother

abuelo - grandfather

ahorita - right now, diminutive form of ahora (now)

amiga - friend (feminine)

arepa - a round, flat cake made of cornmeal in Colombian and Venezuelan cuisines

amor - love

arroz y huevos - rice and eggs

bendiciones - blessings

bruja - witch

caldo - broth, soup

carne asada - grilled steak

chancla - flip-flop, slipper

chingona - badass (feminine)

chingón - fucking great, badass

chismosa - gossiper (feminine)

chocolate espeso - thick chocolate

cierra el pico - shut your mouth/beak

¡como debe de ser! - as it should be!

con - with

corazón - heart

culo - ass

de - of, from

dinero - money

el - the (masculine singular)

en - in

español - Spanish (masculine)

fiesta - party

frijoles - beans

gracias - thank you

guarda tus secretos bien guardados - keep your secrets well kept

guerreras - female warriors

habladores - talkers, gossipers

idiota - idiot

imbécil - imbecile

infeliz - an an unhappy, miserable person

la - the (feminine singular)

las - the (feminine plural)

las perezosas - the lazy ones (feminine)

limón - lemon

lo - it, him

lo bueno y lo malo - the good and the bad

lo que sea - whatever

los - the (masculine plural)

machistas - male chauvinists

Maluma - Colombian rapper and singer-songwriter

mamá - mom

mercado - market

metida - nosy, meddlesome (feminine)

mi - my

mierda - shit

mujeres - women

muy - very

no - no

o - or

palo santo - holy wood

panadería - bakery

para - for

pastelito - little pastry, cupcake

pelos en la lengua - hairs on the tongue (expression meaning "to speak vaguely")

pendeja - idiot, dumbass (feminine)

pendejada - stupidity

pendejo - idiot, dumbass (masculine)

pero - but

poderosa - powerful (feminine)

pollo loco - crazy chicken

por - for, by

por pendeja - for being an idiot/a fool

por poderosa - for being stupid

por si acaso - just in case

puta madre - motherfucker, used as an exclamation of frustration or anger

que - that, what

salvo - except

se - himself, herself, itself, themselves

señora - Mrs., married woman, or older woman

si - if

su - his, her, their, your (formal)

taquito - rolled-up taco

telenovela - novel, soap opera

tía - aunt

tío - uncle

todo - all, everything

¡todo se va a la chingada! - Everything goes to hell!

tóxico - toxic (masculine)

tu - your

un - a (masculine)

una - a (feminine)

uno nunca sabe - you never know

valiente - brave

viejo - old (masculine)

y - and

Acknowledgments

The making of this book was a fast-paced adventure that tested our strengths as first-time authors, advice-givers, and overall tough **mujeres**. It's a deep reflection of our past experiences and lessons learned from those who shaped us and this book alike. We must first thank the top **guerreras**, without whose involvement from day one (a.k.a. the day we were born), we would not have been able to achieve this project: our **mamás.**

To Nidia Aragon, the rock and current matriarch of our family, who never let anyone take her for a **pendeja.** Her tough love and can-do attitude have been invaluable, as well as her support in sharing the proverbial sayings she learned from her ancestors and being the voice from which we found our tone of anti-affirmations.

To Martha Lopez, for being the voice of reason and hard truths when we needed them the most. Her wisdom, humor, and patience all supported the development of the final sayings and tone of this book.

To our **abuelas**, Celmira Aragon and Ercilia Catalina Acosta, the OG matriarchs who gave the most tough love of them all but still gave so much warmth in their own ways and will always be a part of our identities. Celmira, whose tough and sometimes mean demeanor was matched by her intelligence, sharpness, and resilience, from whom we learned independence, strength, and the invaluable gift of sarcastic dry humor. Catalina, whose home was always open and who babysat three generations, was always full of life and energy until her time came. Their sacrifices and blessings have profoundly shaped our families.

To Daliza Garcia, Aralis's sister and Carolina's cousin, a strong, opinionated, and hardworking woman who loves fiercely and stands by her word. She is also an incredible mother to our exceptional niece, Jailyn Ari Garcia. Jailyn, with her wisdom beyond her years and unique Gen-Z perspective, now carries the legacy forward, allowing us to share our family's strength and spirit. Their love has profoundly shaped who we are.

To the men who shaped us alongside our mothers, and who we have to thank for supporting us in more ways than one: Elvis Acosta and Juan Lopez, Carolina's father and stepfather—men who did their absolute best in raising and teaching her throughout the years, and remain two of the most supportive people in her life. Jay Chavez, Aralis's partner—who shows her every day what true love and partnership mean, with endless patience and unwavering support. To our *tío*, Francisco "Pacho" Garcia, who provided his fair share of sayings for the book and always showed us love and humor throughout our childhoods. To Kevin, Carolina's brother and Aralis's cousin—who embodies Celmira's spirit and always gives never-ending love and support, sometimes aggressively but always appreciated. And to Jose Garcia, Aralis's brother-in-law, who has been an older male figure and big brother to her since she was a young teenager. He is a man of his word, direct, and an exemplary father.

We also thank our editorial and publishing team who worked so efficiently and happily to help meet this book's deadline! Special thanks to Avalon Radys, our editor, who tirelessly refined our writing and became an honorary Latina in the process. Thanks to the Blue Star Press team without whom there would be no *Mamá Didn't Raise a Pendeja*, starting with Lindsay Wilkes-Edrington, for launching this project into existence and ensuring we stayed on track with the same tough love we're used to. Big thanks to the rest of the Blue Star team for all their belief in us and their involvement now and in the future— especially Peter Licalzi, Brenna Licalzi, Clare Whitehead, Camden Hendricks, and Bailey Dueitt.

This book would also not be the book it is without our other editors, Becky Bain and Erica Wieczorek, who added sass and edge to our writing. Thanks to the design team—Bryce de Flamand, for working patiently with us to develop the look and feel of the book; and Niege Borges, for the beautiful artwork throughout.

We would never be on the trajectory we are on without the open support of Mike Alfaro, creator of *Millennial Lotería* and who made the introduction to Blue Star Press. He remains our inspiration and motivation to keep supporting the Latino community through products that represent us authentically and in a fun way.

This book is a product of love from so many people, be it through family, friendship, or passion for their craft. Thank you, reader, for taking the time to read through these pages full of voices guiding you to become the best badass version of you.

Carolina Acosta, a Forbes 30 Under 30 lister, is the founder and CEO of Tragos Games, which creates party games that celebrate Latino culture. With a background in graphic and product design, she is dedicated to making beautiful products and authentic experiences that empower the Latino culture. Through Tragos, she has sold over 250,000 copies and raised over $20,000 for causes supporting her community. She currently lives and works remotely in New Jersey, focused on developing more products and spontaneously traveling for fun in between. This is her first book.

Aralis Mejia has a strong background in hospitality, developed in the fast-paced environment of New York City, with a focus on marketing and events. She successfully brought her expertise to Tragos Games, where she has helped amplify the mission of growing cultural games. As the founder of Silara Marketing, Aralis has created an agency that works with businesses of all sizes, helping them strategize and execute integrated marketing plans that blend new technology with traditional tactics. Based in Ridgewood, Queens, Aralis is passionate about elevating Latino culture and supporting her community through effective and innovative marketing. This is her first book.